# Sue Vincent
# Life Lines

## Poems from a Reflection

# Sue Vincent
# Life Lines

Poems from a Reflection

There is a poet in every heart.

# Contents

For the journey...
And those who share it.

# Purpose

The pen paints the souls longing
In jewel tones.
Darkness veils the stars,
Yet their Light shines unseen,
But not unfelt;
An ember of gold
In the shadows.
Now you remind us
To count all our blessings,
Holding them dear
For the little while.
You remind us too
That chivalry survives,
And the courage to laugh
In the face of tragedy.
Then you remind us
That friendship is precious
A gift to be cherished
And never lost.
I am reminded
That life has its purpose
And our purpose in life
Is to Live it.

# Maya

Do I cease to exist if I am not seen,
Like a tree in a forest that makes no sound
Unless it is heard when it falls?
Do I exist in the mirror when I look,
An illusory glimpse into a framed reality
That is not real?
Viewer or image, who can say
Where reality resides
Or if we are but dreaming?
Is my life a mere illusion of the soul
Or perhaps a whispered image
In the mind of God?
Or is illusion's self the fount,
Imagined solidity
Becoming real with every heartbeat?
If I am forgotten, was I ever there?
Did I leave my trace upon a world
Whose reality I question
Or was I just a zephyr
In the cosmic night
Whispered to the stars
By voiceless lips…
Or did I touch your heart?

# Seasons

The past drags its feet,
Backwards, away,
Fading from memory
Half remembered.
The present, needle sharp,
Reminds us of its presence;
Insistent clamour
At the door of vision.
The future tantalizes;
Glimpses half seen,
Pages that wait for our hand
To write the next chapter....
Life threads twining
Snake-like about each other;
A lovers knot
Tied around eternity.

# Drink the Dawn

Society demands we do our best;
Striving, trying for the common goal,
The home, the car, the holiday…
Squeezing ourselves into a mould
Shaped by the grey people,
The tax collectors,
The nine to fivers
Caught by fear of failure
And bound by convention.
That is their safety net
Seeking justification
For their insecurities
In the reflection
Of our compliance.
I want to do my worst,
To give life all I've got,
To break the rules,
Twisting them and making sausage dogs
Of their inflated importance
Like a Fool with a balloon.
To dive into sunsets
And drink the dawn
From an empty cup,
Laughing in the morning.
Will you join me in a sunrise?

# I See You…

It is in the high places and wild spaces I see you.
There I hear your laughter echo in the hills,
Dancing on the mist, a will o' the wisp with joyous grace,
Challenging the wind to chase you
And kiss your face.

I see you on the seashore, running through the waves
Barefoot in a winter sea, being a child because you can,
Leaving your cares abandoned at the water's edge
Discarded like the shoes you left
Behind you on the sand.

I see you walking underneath the winter trees,
Leaving footprints in the sodden emerald moss
Frozen, fragile glass beneath your feet
As you speak of life and memory
And I watch you change.

I find you in the winter land, in snowy silence.
As a year turns, graced with tears that know no grief
And time falls from your face, forgotten trace
Of another past. I watch your eyes
Remember childhood's flame.

# Flowers

There were flowers.
Orchids pinned upon a mother's breast,
All lace and diamonds,
Long black gloves
And painted lips,
A child that watched
As she left laughing
When the door closed.

There were flowers,
Yellow tulips,
Cellophane and ribbon
And a girl who blushed
As the curtain fell
Upon the stage
As she cradled them.
A first bouquet.

There were flowers,
Roses and lilies
White, in hands and hair,
Their fragrance mingled
With frankincense,
A ghost of awe and wonder
Finding a home
In memory.

There were flowers..
Rainbow hued,
Everywhere.
Greeting a life newborn,
Gifts of love and welcome
Lighting the stark severity
Of the room
As a babe cried.

There were flowers,
Daisy chains
Wound around his brow
Crowning him
In the sunlight
In laughter,
In simplicity,
In love.

There were flowers,
Three red roses,
Red as life,
Placed in a cold hand,
One for each heart
Saying a final farewell.

When the tears fall,
There are always flowers.

# In Sorrow's Depths

In sorrow's depths hides a spark of Light,
Seemingly untouchable, unattainable.
Tears blind your eyes to it,
Pain blinds your heart,
Memory enshrouds you,
Pulling you down
Into the abyss.
Hold out your hand,
The light will not burn you,
Nor flee if you seize it.
It only grows in brightness
As you move towards it,
Warming your heart
With the hearth-fire glow,
Blending the shadows
On night's canvas
Till the stars appear.

# Lady in White

She takes the cloak out of its wrappings,
Stored for years against the moths and dust
Of accumulated inactivity.
The satin weight of fur slides through her fingers
Like the memories it holds
Caught, immobile for a moment
Within its pristine folds.
There is no photograph to share,
She was not captured
High upon the cliff or in the cavern,
Salt spray on her lips
And sea-thrift in her hair
Playing with the wind as the sun rose.
Cloaked in memory, as in the fabric folds,
She walked in silent wonder
At the death-in-life encompassed,
Contemplating new beginnings held in endings,
Bound by a blood stained cord.
It binds her still.
Deeper than the ocean that she gazed upon,
A single thread of evanescent Light
That winds about her then, her now,
Entwined with her tomorrow
And all about her falls the snowy mantle,
Weighty folds enshroud her
As she remembers who she was and will become,
Lady in White.

# You are Loved

Three words felt, not spoken,
Known only in the inmost heart
That change the world
And how you see it.
It doesn't matter who
Or how, or where.
Time and distance have no meaning,
When you Know it.
Nor do the source or reasons count.
It is not tied to town or place,
To country, friend or single face.
It flows through Being,
Owned by none and all
Without distinction.
And when its doors are opened
By the smallest breeze
Eternity comes in
And wraps around you
From a single Source
And you are Loved.

# Golden

There is a place on dawn's horizon
Where the heart breathes
In the gold of morning
Drinking sunlight in the dew.
An unknown land,
A journey of becoming,
Beyond the world,
Beyond eternity,
Where time rules nothing
And a hundred years
Are but a thought away.
They wait for you,
Gilded memories
Of futures past
And endless dawning,
Casting shadows at your feet,
In the brightness
That lights your path.
Hands reach out
To hold you
And guide your step
In loving welcome,
Drawing you home.
And you are golden.

# Benediction

Risen flame gilds the clouds as I greet the sun.
Rooted in earth, my vision filled with beauty,
I offer my pain to the Lords of Light,
And see it consumed.
I place my fears in the crucible
And watch them burn.
Flame melts to opalescence;
The benediction of a luminous dawn.

# A Dark Night

Soft, velvet darkness,
Pierced with the brilliance
Of diamond stars.
Vaulted Temple to the Comely One,
Womb of the Goddess
Silence unbroken
Except by Her heartbeat.
A cocoon of rebirth.
Canvas for the colours of Heaven
Perfect foil for their glory,
Asking nothing
Save that we behold It
With understanding.

# Paper Wings

In sleepless silence
night mourns the dreaming
lost to a fallen star.
Shadows chase the ghosts of morning,
ever seeking to consume them,
jealous of their light.
Paper wings flutter
unheeded to the floor
in flightless death.
The wakeful poet dips his pen
in cold coffee
beside the empty bed
and yearns for dawn.

# Calling

I whispered your name to the Universe
Silent echoes, butterflies on the wind,
Calling you to me.
Only in softness, gentle as snowflakes,
Fragile and transient
Will the voiceless speak.
Yet into the silence your name flutters,
A feather falling at my feet
From a clear sky.
I hear my voice and listen to my own cry
Calling your name in the silence
In you I find myself

# Silence

In a silence broken only by breath
Words lose their sound;
Spill their essence on the pristine page
Or curl in tendrils through a mind undone,
Fleeing logic on wings of fantasy.
Fabled spectres rear their heads,
Horned dilemmas bow before a ghost
Of newborn Understanding,
Mewling helpless in a night
Of infant shadows.
The dreamer dreams the song,
Seeking music in a voice,
A poem in the starlit dark
To break the silence
And give birth to sound.
Muted whispers kiss the soul
That stays to listen in the darkness
Reaching for the Word it almost hears
Until it knows the only sound
Is life's first breath
Sighing in the silence.

# A Mother's Hands

I see my mother's hands before my eyes
The first caress that I had ever known,
And with a thrill of wonder realise
The hands I see before me are my own.
Where did the decades go? I have to ask.
At what point did my springtime slip away?
Is this mid-summer sun in which I bask
Or has the autumn brought a shorter day?
A mellowing has softened me, I know,
Yet coloured me with richer hue and shade,
And written on my face a map to show
The world the choices I have made.
I too can read the story as I look
Of all the things of which I am a part,
The journey traced in lines upon the book
Within the mirror of an open heart.
There read the fearless laughter of the child,
The joys and grief, the lovers I have known,
The windswept glory of a heart gone wild,
The maiden's tears, the mother's love, the crone.
But as I journey on and turn the page
Not knowing what will come or what will be,
Or even if true wisdom comes with age,
I see adventure beckoning to me.
I know my winter holds a longer night
And seasons turn for all things on this earth,
The snowy shroud will cover all in white
That it may sleep, and there await rebirth.

# No Other Way?

A chill flame burns in the hearth
Where the embers of warmth
Should smoulder golden
In the morning
Carrying the gentle night
To a new dawn.
Dew falls, salt and bitter
On the sapling
Torn from earth
To become a spear
Launched to flight,
Seeking its prey
With a hunter's hunger.
What of the branch
Where the songbirds rest
Singing to the sun
Amid the flowers?
What of the fruits;
Its berries, drops of blood
From a prey too strong to die,
Stain the hunter's hand
With the shame of destruction
And the madness of knowing
No other way.

# Remember

Cold creeps in slowly,
Bones, chilled and brittle
Snap like twigs,
Fragile and friable.
Remembered warmth
Turns the mind to memory;
Sunlight and laughter
And your hand in mine
Murmuring dreams;
Walking our future
As our words entwine
And our hearts race
Seeing the far yesterday
In our tomorrow.
Climbing our mountains
With the innocence of children,
Finding our future
In each other's eyes.

# Midnight Haiku

### #1

Walk lightly upon the earth.
There is no weight in shadows,
Nor scales in the heart

### #2

There is no escape from fear
Save to meet it face to face
With understanding.

### #3

Beauty bows its head with grace
Tears fill the heart of the rose;
Summer bids farewell.

# Vale of tears

Shards of naivety strew the path;
Calloused feet, weary and wary,
Sliced by broken dreams
And shattered rainbows
Trudge onward,
Leaving bloody traces
In the innocence
Of a martyred dream.
Those who cross the vale of tears
Come not again so lightly,
But tread with care
Preserving solitude
Against the pain
Of other feet they cannot heal
With words or touch;
Offering their footprints,
Scarlet on white,
To guide their steps
To the Beginning.

# Waterfall

Footprints in snow trace an echo of longing,
Ghosts on a Dancing Floor paved black and white
Waltzing in silence through deep drifting Roses;
Memories dance in the Garden tonight.

The Tower looks on with its ever-blind windows
Whispering fantasies wander the Halls
Naked and caged there a Lover lies bleeding,
Beauty enchanted and chained in its Walls.

Hung from the bridge that could lead to salvation,
Under the Moon with a Star in his Eye,
Flashes the Blade that will bring him to freedom
Holding the gaze that will teach him to Fly.

The Castle lies silent, the wind mourns the laughter,
The Pool now reflects but a summer in flames
Yet under the hill where the Sun guards a Shadow
A shimmering waterfall whispers their Names.

# Growing Season

Is there time enough to walk the landscape of the heavy heart
When springtime's pastures beckon and adventure calls?
Should we run laughing out to greet them in the morning light
Or close the door behind us to an empty hall?
And should not summer's warmth be full of brighter sun
Not shadowed by regret for what has flown?
Can we not sit and wonder at a butterfly
Instead of longing for the things we might have known?
When autumn riches settle on a fertile land
Must we look back and hanker for the spring?
Can we see nothing in the tree that bears the fruit
Or only dream of what elusive youth could bring?
In winter when the shrouded world is half asleep
Should we see nothing in the dancing firelight
But ghosts of yesterday and might-have-been
Illusions of a past that memory paints bright?
Walk lightly through the seasons as they turn and dance
The past is naught, tomorrow still unseen
And fall in love with life at every passing day,
For what you think you are, you will have been.

# Odin's Ravens

As night draws in and silence comes,
The door is locked, the curtains drawn
I am alone, the world recedes
And sleeps until another dawn.
Yet in the quiet, midnight hour
Feathers soft against my skin
Two ravens whisper in my ear,
As Thought and Memory begin.

Within the darkness of their wings
Stir images, both dark and bright,
That dance within the secret heart
And quiet hours of the night.
A past replayed, as on a screen,
As tears and laughter, broken dreams,
And in their midst a single spark,
A star of quiet beauty gleams.

Deep in its central molten core,
From what has been the present grows
A seed that reaches to the sun,
And borrowing its light it glows
With inner glory, burning bright,
With all the mornings yet to be,
The future held within the wings
Of ravens, Thought and Memory.

# Sunset

The sun set tonight. It always does.
A blaze of glory in the western sky, closing the day.

Did you see the flames caress the moon as she rose?
Or were you sleeping, dreaming of survival.
It will not come again, that moment.
Once missed it is forever gone.

There are stars tonight, a faint light in the heavens.
Almost drowned by the glow of cities, yet ever present on the edge of
vision, scattered motes of possibility in the darkness.

Dawn will follow. It always does.
A gentle birthing in the eastern sky.
Will you greet the sun?
Watch the delicate petals unfold a new beginning?
It will not come again.
Not *this* dawn.

Will you take this virgin morn and make it yours?
Or will you sleep?

# Now

I am not the 'I' I was,

Nor the 'I' I shall become,

I am,

*Now,*

Present,

Only in this moment.

# Turning

Snowflakes of memory fall
Kissing the gentle night,
Melting on my skin
In the moonlight.
I remember winter,
Sunlight on frozen hills
When I sought summer
In the pale eyes of spring,
And found the gold of autumn
Waiting in the silence
As the seasons turned.

# Dreaming

I dreamed you last night.
You were the heart that listened to my fears,
Comforting the pain with tea and tissues
And attentive ears.

You were there with me as I faced them,
Slaying them one by one, with logic and laughter,
And a belief in me that I had forgotten,
Lost in the morass that pulled me down.

I saw you sitting there, hands around the cup,
Eyes holding me steady, as I remembered
All that I have been, all I can be,
All I will become.

But you were many things.
And I saw father, mother, sibling, every lover,
Playmate, teacher, every friend, I ever knew,
And so much more, that in the end I realised
That you were I, and I was you,
A mirrored soul, both one, yet two,
And then you shared my joy.

# Forget-me-not

My eyes watch in your heart, you know their colours,
Flags that fly emotions as a signal to the world,
A secret language you alone can read
Even when I close them.

You do not forget.
You know each line and curve of lips,
You know their taste and torment,
Understand their passion
Even in my absence you will not forget.

You know my skin, remember how it quivered
At the thought of yours, and how it feels,
A yielding softness, pillowing your head
Upon my heartbeat, you cannot forget.

You know my heart, a secret archive
Of experience and dreams, fragile marble,
Galatea, finding life in love
With each shared breath. How could you forget?

I know your smile, the one that is my own,
That stripped the years away from you
And all your care, just children playing,
And your eyes laughing.

I will remember.

# Just a shell

It's just a shell.
Small but perfect,
Picked up on the beach that day.
Its sits beside the little stone you found,
Children hand in hand
Along a winter shore.

It's just a shell.
Nothing very special
There were hundreds of them
Washed up on the beach that way
Strewn across the sand
When the tide came.

It's just a shell
A hollow thing
And empty, just a memory
Of a gifted day
Beside the waves.
I have it still

It's just a shell.
It sits within my hand
I hear our laughter
Dancing in the windswept dunes
And smile through tears
And face the day…
Just a shell.

# Wishing

I close my eyes
And the wind in the trees
Sounds like the sea.
Valleys have held me too long
Smothered by manicured fields
And anonymous houses.

My soul craves the high place
Of childhood and memory;
Last year's bracken
And tomorrow's heather,
The chatter of a pure stream
And the graven rocks
Hanging from an iron sky.

And the sea…
Heart-beat of earth,
Mirroring the heavens,
Shifting like the wind
That sings in the trees.

# Tonight

There is a cold place in my heart tonight
Where the beauty of life
Is overlaid with sadness
And the fear of loss.

Where hope has diminished,
A small spark of brightness
In a surly night.

Where the laughter of friends
Is hushed in the silence,
And a cry in the dark
Rends the heart, helpless.

There is hope still
In miracles,
But slender and fading.
The smallest thing.

And the knowledge of challenge,
Another dragon,
Another mountain to climb
And I am weary.

Send me your gift,
The memory of laughter
Shared in joy
And a friend's embrace.

## Secret, molten core

I know so little of the world,
Save what there is to know in love.
I have not seen.
Yet you who have walked it
Do you know it?
Have you seen with eyes that see
The beauty of a morning?
Or a crocus pierce the snow,
Opening its heart
To the sun's birthing?
Have you touched
The secret, molten core
That fire, glowing unregarded
In the inner self?
Ah Beloved,
In this faded room,
Where solitude holds silence,
Companionship a dreaming,
Here the world is mine,
Because I see it,
And I am free
Because I will it so.
The tides of passion
Wash around my feet,
I will not stand upon the shore
A mere observer
But will drown in them.
I have chosen.

# The Spinner

She sits and spins,
A tapestry of wonders
Taking shape and life
Between her vision
And her words.

Her mind a world away
From errant children setting out
To carry the spark of life
To a new dawning.
And yet, within that spark
Her fire blooms.

A wildflower sown and rooted
In their souls.
Grown in love,
Watered with tears ,
Nurtured with laughter
And cherished wisdom.

Looking back
As the tide takes them,
Her children see only the distant beacon
Of a mother's love.

# Dance

There is a single thread,
That runs through every life,
And binds us at the heart.

A web of life so intricate and fine,
A spider silk of spirit
With tensile strength to carry any grief
And share all joy.

Holding us with love
As we journey…
Together and alone.

Momentary touches
Woven and interweaving
Many and One
In a single dance.

## Goodnight

Tonight I am weary,
Cold sleeplessness
A mind in motion
And a voice in the silence
Held to attention
In the darkness.

But tonight I will sleep.
Emotion has cleansed me
Clean wind in the heart
And a distant goodnight
Carried to my bedside
In a moment's care
To ease the stillness
With a friend's laughter.

Tonight I sleep
As the world grows wings
And learns to fly
Into the morning
Singing the dawn.

# Points of View

Some eyes see only through a darkened haze
With cataracts and blinkers, self-conditioned;
Blind to the dancing joy where rainbows arc,
Afraid to see the colours life commissioned.

Some eyes see far in pastel coloured glory;
Leaving life behind them as they sail
Upon a golden mist of wonder in the morning
To reach a world that glows behind the veil.

Some eyes look inwards, seeing only self,
Or mirrored images of other eyes;
Colouring their vision with their fears,
They live in hope that every mirror lies.

Some eyes are dull and lifeless, hold no light,
No spark within, of happiness bereft,
All joy extinguished by the flow of tears
As sorrow weighs the pittance they have left.

Some see with certainty in monochrome
In black or white there is no compromise,
No shade of grey compassion in their glance,
No empathy or kindness in their eyes.

Yet some illuminate the world they see,
And some eyes burn with passionate desire,
Some hold the lambent argent of the seer
That radiate a visionary fire.

But there are those that simply look with love
They view the world with pure serenity;
Within both dark and bright discover joy
And innocent, they see as children see.

In these eyes you may see a soul reflected
Held safe in beauty in another's view,
Look deep and take the gift of other's seeing,
The soul into whose eyes you gaze is you.


## Just for a Moment

Let me see your face, just for a moment
Lit by the moonlight through the window
Before I close my eyes in sleep
Give me your dreams, Beloved,
And I will weave them for you
On the loom of a nascent sunrise
While you sleep on my pillow
With your arms around me
Here you are the Dreamer
And I am the Weaver
Warp and weft
Of a single
Pattern
Called
Love

# What is love?

What is love?
Is it the comfort of a touch when the night is cold?
Or knowing that whatever comes there is a hand to hold?
The feeling, too much for words, of togetherness
When heart speaks to heart in simple tenderness?
Is it the journey, day after day of small silly things
When each humble service is joy and your heart just sings?
Or one love, many faceted, jewel-like, casting rainbows
Illuminating the dark and hidden places that lurk in the mind.
One love, ebbing and flowing through consciousness,
Pulsing with every heartbeat renewed with every breath.
One love, born of joy and shared humanity,
Grown in the womb of the Universe
Nurtured at Its breast.
One love, greater than fear, vanquishing death
With the white Light of immortality.
One love, unending and ceaseless
All that we are
Crystallised diamond bright
In a single smile.

# Direction

I whisper you to the west,
The mist carried your name across the cloud-path,
Coursing through the life blood of rivers,
Washing far off shores as tides ebb and flow,
Drawn by the moonlight.

I whispered you to the south,
The sun shone for you, gilding your hair,
Sand devils danced with the serpents before you
Passionate abandon of summer
In a painted desert.

I whispered you to the east,
The breeze took you, caressing your skin
Kissing your face as you laughed in the sunrise
Filling your being with breath
In jealous intimacy.

I whispered you to the north,
Where the hills curve around you like a lover,
Undulating gently beneath your body
Pressed close to her green mantle
As the sky darkens for you.

I whispered you to my soul
Your name echoed in the star filled void
I found there. And every star was you
And also I, and something more
Reflecting only Love.

## Just One

How many loves to fill a heart?
Many, perhaps, or just one at the end?
Love for a mother's smile, golden in childhood,
Unbroken illusion of happiness
That persists in memory.
The love of a first kiss, delicate, tremulous,
Mingling fear and excitement in awkward embrace
And discovered delight.
The love of a lifetime, dreamed in confetti, veiled in lace,
Sparkling like the diamond on its finger
In the moonlight.
Or love conceived,
Silent miracle that grows in silence,
Born to be loved, and growing in laughter
Drying tears in your hair even when he has to bow down
Just to reach.
Then the love of a friend,
With whom you share joy and run to in pain
And shared trust, without barriers.
Or the loves who are lost,
Heart aching absence, the unending counterpoint
That shadows joy… the heart's chiaroscuro.
Or loves we are losing,
The vision of absence glazes each day
With future pain, while the soul keens softly.
How many loves to fill a heart?
Many, I think…or just one.
The love of Life despite present pain
Or future grief, regardless of memory
Dark or bright.

Embracing the sadness and the joy
That make us whole and tears us apart
Rebuilding us in Light.
How many loves to fill a heart?
To make it overflow with joy
And break it ceaselessly with recurring pain,
Healing it with laughter and a gentle smile?
Just One.


## Empty Vessel

I am empty;
Serving no purpose until I am filled.
Born to give shape and form
To that which fills me.
A vessel of Light awaiting a word
And the hand that pours the wine of Life
Into my waiting.
Insubstantial, it is my substance
Into which the waters flow,
Held in safety, preserved from dissipation
By the cup of my being.
My feet in earth
Lips raised to the sky in joyful paean,
Catching heaven's rain as it falls
And fills me with its clarity
That I may drink the morning.

# What can you see?

What can you see when you read me?
Do you see the wind in my hair
And my feet in the heather
And hear me laugh as the grouse rise?
Can you feel my awe as the storm breaks?
Hurtling overhead
As the old gods wage war
Amid the clouds?
When you looked, did you see the smile?
Painted in place for protection,
Hiding the scars on my face
And those in my heart.
Shrouded in false joy against questions
I could not answer
And would not face
That haunted me.
And deeper, behind the veil,
Could you see pain?
Laughter played its part
And hid my heart from prying eyes,
A place of my own to crouch in,
Behind a mask
Where few would look,
Or think to see.
Look deeper yet, for there was more.
Serenity hard won,
Balanced on a knife edge
Striving for equilibrium
Yet pulled and torn,
Twixt grief and joy.

Always searching
Blinkered.
Now look again, for I have changed
A blade immolated
In a strange, new furnace
Emerging re-forged
With a flame, a passion
Burning within.
Tell me, what can you see?
For I do not know.

## Memory

My fingers traced your skin in curve and line,
My touch the eyes of memory as you slept
Warm against my skin and breathing softly,
In the sunlight.

My pillow held the hollow where you lay,
With love glazed eyes that held me,
Watching as the wildness took me,
Smiling up at me.

I lay my head within that hollow space
An unmade bed my keepsake of the night,
The fantasy of skin and loving lingers
Calling my tears.

# Rising

The bed is cold, and empty.
Only oblivion beckons,
Only dreaming.
No-one whispers there
Or speaks a name
Into the darkness.
The moon is full tonight
Smiling down on lovers.
Lightly veiled,
Silvered curves of skin
Entwined in tenderness.
Yet here she casts but shadows,
Phantom presence
Mirroring a dream,
A longing unfulfilled
A fire kindled
And unquenched,
Consuming night
With velvet gloves
And starlit promises
Of languid mornings
When the sunlight
Sees the hawk rise,
Taking flight into the dawn
That gave him birth
And calls him home
To immolation
In the heart's flame.
Willing sacrifice of self,
Unresisting gallantry,
With eyes that hold the vision

Of beyond the veil.
He is no victim.
Yet as his torment burns him
Darkness turns to ashes,
Drifting on the wind.
Tempered, forged in pain
A tender alchemy of Love
That leaves him only joy
And golden life
And laughter in the morning
Rising with the mist
As he takes flight.

# I

I am not real. I never was.
The wind blows, carrying me like a winter leaf.

Fragile, I hold life in my hands;
I have no life of my own.
Life carries me where it wills,
My choices are not mine to make.
Yet I hold the Keys.

I am the Gate of Life and Portal of Death.
Eternity is my gift.
I mirror the world and am, myself, its reflection;
Unreachable, unreal.
Separate from the stream.

None touch me, and all.

Am I the courage to follow a dream?

I go where I am sent.
Unchanging, I bring change.
Both cause and catalyst.

Change follows my touch, blood behind the scalpel,
For good or ill, I do not know,
Nor may I stay to see the end.
But pay the price in pain.

I fly through dream.
I walk the nightmare alone,
Terrifying semblance of reality,
A landscape of hooded hills.
A conquered mountain, a shrouded vale unknowable.
Ghouls taunt me, shadows of Self,
Echoed in vision.

My masks are many,
None knows them all, even I.
Some own a mask, believe they hold me
But I hide in laughter and hunger, waiting.

My time is not yet,
And has always been now.
I am a dream, a fantasy,
Smoke in a sunbeam, elusive.
Joy and pain render me visible,
Yet both are tenuous,
Fragile as snow, shadows in the glass.

I am not real. I never was.

## Rombald's Moor

hor2Tall the cliffs of stone
That mark the entry to my heart's domain,
Wild and empty in its vastness
The solitude of living earth.
The wind lifts the heart
And bears it through the storm
To where the lichen crusted rocks
Cling to the clouds.
Part of my heart remains there
Scattered with the ashes of a lost love
Mingled with the joy and pain of memory,
Of childhood wonder and a lover's kiss.
Deep the roots which bind me to that land,
Like the weathered pines that cling for life
To the purple hillside…
Genuflecting, but standing, still,
Naked in the mist.
Or the great stones,
Ice carved in aeons past
Into a landscape of dreams,
Marked by ancient hands
With figures of Light,
That I may stand beside them,
Millennia apart,
And recognise my kin.

## Ma Quête

*J'ai cherché sans te trouver,*
*Dans les étoiles qui scintillent*
*Et les ténèbres profondes*
*Sans te voir.*
*Je te croyais fantôme,*
*Image de l'espoir,*
*Né du désire,*
*Ephémère comme la brume*
*Ou mon rêve.*
*Je ne savais pas*
*Que tu y étais déjà,*
*Ame de mon âme*
*Qui m'attendais*
*Au fond du cœur*


I sought without finding
In the shimmering stars
And the deep shadows
And saw you not.
I thought you a phantom,
Image of hope,
Born of desire,
Ephemeral as the mist
Or my dream.
I knew not
That you were already here,
Soul of my soul,
Waiting for me
In the depths of my heart.

# Bedwyr's Song

On the dark road to midnight
The bard takes his rest
With a song in his dream
And his heart on the Quest.
The hollow hills beckon,
The call of the Fae…
The Light in his heart burns
To show him the Way.

To the stone by the well,
In the green, leafy glade,
With the stars on the Water
Reflecting the Blade.
There Mother and Maiden
Will hold up the Grail,
Be true and your questing,
Sir Knight, cannot fail.

'Tis only the purest in heart, it is told,
With an innocent faith, in his soul,
Who can follow the Path through the darkest of nights,
To the Castle that shelters his goal.
Though the wildwood bewilders his stumbling feet
The Knight marches onward and true,
Through bramble and thicket he forges ahead
With his Vision his hearts only view.

On the shores of a Lake
Our Knight stops to rest,
Where once, for a King
As a final request,

He had taken a Blade
Wrought of glory and pain,
Cast it far in the Lake
To conceal it again.

For the glory had failed
And the story had died,
Pierced with a darker Blade
Deep in its side.
There the Blood that had fallen,
The Life that was shed,
Rekindled the Heart
Of the Land where he bled.

As the dawn rises over the dark, glassy Lake
On the shore, where the mistwraiths arise,
The incense of apple wood perfumes the air,
And the morning Light shines from his eyes…
The Veil thins, revealing the prow of a boat
That sailed to him thus once before,
When the Blade that was forged out of magic and Light
He had cast, in his grief, from the shore.

Then the barge had appeared
As the Hand took the Sword
And the Queens had enfolded
His sacrificed Lord.
Yet, this time is different,
For there in the prow
The Lady is smiling
And beckons him now.

He crosses the water,

The song of the Quest
Echoes the drum beating
Deep in his breast.
The Mists close around him
No longer to roam,
For Avalon's Lady
Is taking him Home.


## Fools Gold

It's a farce, of course;
This worship of Mammon
And the daily grind
That numbs the senses
And warps the mind.
Rainbow chasing.
Devoid of style,
Kicking and screaming
The Golden Mile
Beckons insidiously.
Pyrite glitter
Blinding our eyes
To the hungry child
Beleaguered by flies.
And we cry charity,
Shed a false tear
And brandish the plastic
To save us the trouble
Of anything drastic...
Like being human.

# Yours...

Yours were the lips that breathed against mine,
Sharing the warmth of desire in the darkness
Sharing the chill of a winters morning, laughing,
Like children, untrammelled by fear
Or the mendacities of survival.

Yours was the touch that opened me to fire,
To the conflagration of self, the immolation of passion
On an altar of self-sacrifice and world denial,
Willing victim of the deepest blaze,
Consuming consummation.

Yours were the eyes, burning like ice
That bound me in flame and warped my perception,
Focusing my vision on the single point of your heart,
Blinding me with tomorrows that drew me inwards,
Drowning in the moment's purity.

Yours was the joy of tender awakenings,
Feathered caresses in the dawn glow of slumber,
Golden in the mornings with the suns kiss,
Jealous of the shadows that hid your face
Beneath the duvet.

# Door of Dreams

Would you walk the corridor of dreams,
Into the dark and unknown inner places,
Where silent voices whisper your desires
From unkissed lips upon amorphous faces?

Dare you cross the Temple chequerboard,
Where black and white in alternating tread
Reflect the hope and terror of the night,
To face imaginations deepest dread?

Could you face each inner world you find,
Knowing that they are a true reflection
That show the turmoil of the conscious mind
Destroying your illusion of perfection?

Can you face the demons hidden there,
Where every rock and tree and fragrant flower,
May hold the cryptic kernel of your fears
Reverberating with emotive power?

Look deep into the mirror of your dreams
To see reflected ancient joys and sorrow,
Begin to read the soul that journeys there
And face today and walk toward tomorrow.

# Amazed

We walk the cosmic labyrinth
In sanctity and grace,
An interwoven farandole
Where each soul has its place.
A cosmic tree, where every fruit
In serpents coil is caught,
And every walker joins a dance
Whose steps are learned, not taught.
A stately, ordered chaos
Where the parts make up the whole,
Tells step, by intertwining step,
The journey of the soul.

## About the Author

Sue Vincent is a Yorkshire born writer, esoteric teacher and Director of The Silent Eye. She has been immersed in the Mysteries all her life. Sue maintains a popular blog Daily Echo at www.scvincent.com and is the author of *The Osiriad* and *Sword of Destiny*. Sue lives in Buckinghamshire, having been stranded there some years ago due to an accident with a blindfold, a pin and a map. She has a lasting love-affair with the landscape of Albion, the hidden country of the heart. She is currently owned by a small dog who also blogs.

The friendship of Sue Vincent and Stuart France has a peculiar alchemy of humour, scholarship and vision that has given birth to several books, including the Doomsday Series and the Triad of Albion: *The Initiate, Heart of Albion* and *Giants Dance*.

The Silent Eye is a modern Mystery School that seeks to allow its students to find the inherent magic in living and being. With students around the world the School offers a fully supervised and practical correspondence course that explores the self through guided inner journeys and daily exercises. It also offers workshops that combine sacred drama, lectures and informal gatherings to bring the teachings to life in a vivid and exciting format. Full details of the School may be found on the official website: www.thesilenteye.co.uk

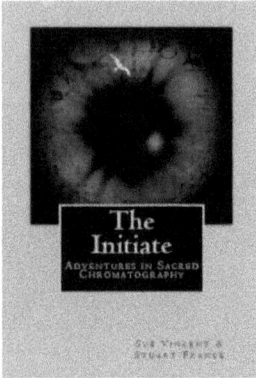

# THE INITIATE:

## Adventures in Sacred Chromatography

## Sue Vincent & Stuart France

### Foreword by Steve Tanham

*Book One of the Triad of Albion*

Imagine wandering through an ancient landscape wrought in earth and stone, exploring the sacred sites of peoples long ago and far away in time and history. The mounds and barrows whisper legends of heroes and magic, painted walls sing of saints and miracles and vision seeps through the cracks of consciousness.

Now imagine that the lens of the camera captures a magical light in soft blues and misty greens and gold. A light that seems to have no cause in physical reality. What would you do?

If you were open to the possibility of deeper realities, perhaps you would wish to explore this strange phenomenon...something two people came to know as sacred chromatography.

The Initiate is the story of just such a journey beyond the realms of our accustomed normality. It is a factual tale told in a fictional manner. In this way did the Bards of old hide in the legends and deeds of heroes those deeper truths for those who had eyes to see and ears to hear.

As the veils thin and waver, time shifts and the present is peopled with the shadowy figures of the past, weaving their tales through a quest for understanding and opening wide the doors of perception for those who seek to see beyond the surface of reality.

Over 60 Full Colour Illustrations

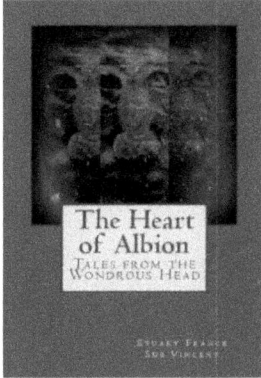

# THE HEART OF ALBION:

## Tales from the Wondrous Head

## Stuart France & Sue Vincent

*Book Two of the Triad of Albion*

**"If I am consciously following a woman who is about to engage a Llama in conversation, which I certainly appear to be, it does not impinge too negatively upon my thought processes."**

What do Jack and the Beanstalk have to do with a spiritual quest? What, for that matter, is the nature of the relationship between Salome and the Jester? Why is Wen conversing with a llama in the Yorkshire Dales? And what links the beautiful and sacred landscape that is the Heart of Albion with Breakfast in Slug Town? These, and many other questions, must be considered as Don and Wen continue the journey begun in The Initiate exploring the shadowy roots of the ancient myths and legends of these Blessed Isles, steering a perilous path through the murky waters of religious symbolism and iconography.

**"Breakfast in Slug Town?"**

Join them on their continuing quest for knowledge and understanding as they explore the landscape of England and people it with strange creatures and even stranger theories, using sacred intent and guided imagination to penetrate into the mysteries unfolding before them.

Illustrated in full colour throughout

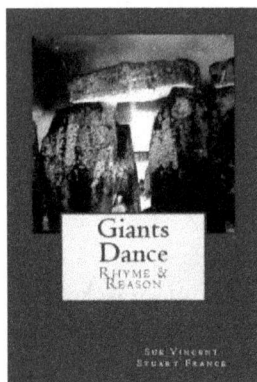

# GIANTS DANCE:

## Rhyme and Reason

## Stuart France and Sue Vincent

*Book Three of the Triad of Albion*

It began with a walk over the bracken covered hillsides of Derbyshire to a lonely stone circle, almost forgotten. It was just a walk...until the hawk flew from the tree and once again the visions began.

Plunged into a realm beyond reality, further than history, deeper than time, Don and Wen begin to unravel the hidden messages hidden in plain sight, concealed by habit and acceptance, and extraordinary magic framed within the small things of ordinary life.

Follow a journey across the Heart of Albion and become an Initiate of the mysterious verity of verse.

*"Interesting that they should seek to make the seven four like that."*

*"Three harmonic pairs and a jubilant head?"*

*"It reminds me of something biblical."*

*"It wouldn't be Jubilees would it? The Hebrews, you know, took an awful lot with them when they fled from Egypt."*

*"I know, but it's not Jubilees, although that does bear some consideration. It's the three-score years and ten! It's precisely the same dynamic. In fact, we even raised the question of whether there was anything in the tradition appertaining to it."*

*"And now we have our answer!"*

*"The Hebrew's Divinely sanctioned earthly span of life is determined by the Seven Hathors."*

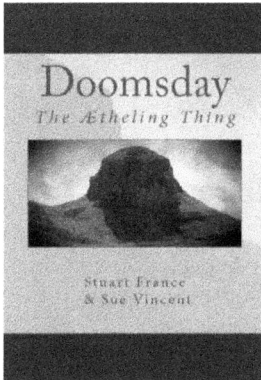

Book One of the Doomsday Triad

# Doomsday: The Ætheling Thing

## Stuart France & Sue Vincent

"Who was this Arviragus bloke anyway?"

Don studies the light as it plays through his beer, casting prisms on the table. How is it possible to hide such a story... the hidden history of Christianity in Britain? Oh, there are legends of course... old tales... Yet what if there was truth in them? What was it that gave these blessed isles such a special place in the minds of our forefathers? There are some things you are not taught in Sunday School.

\*\*\*

"Get this... 'ætheling from O.E. Æpling, 'son of a king, man of royal blood, nobleman, chief, prince, king, Christ, God-Man, Hero, Saint...'"
"Wait a minute... wait a minute... give me that last bit again."
"...Christ, God-Man, Hero, Saint..."
"Didn't we call our Arthur, Aeth in, 'The Heart of Albion'?"
"We did."
"And didn't we set his story in Mercia?"
"We did."
"Well that's it then...The Anglo Saxon kings were claiming divine descent."
"That's true, but the Anglo-Saxon kings' descent wasn't from God it was from Christ."
"And how did they get there?"
"They got there from their very own High One who also hung from a tree with a spear in his side... screaming."
"Odin!"
"They evidently regarded Christ as an avatar of Odin."
"Blimey, you'll not read that in any history book!"
"Just as well we're not writing a history then isn't it?"

*Book Two of the Doomsday Triad*

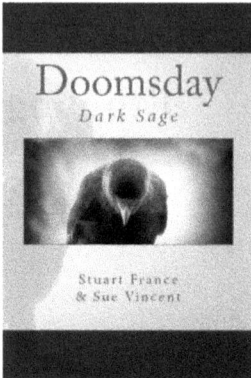

# Doomsday: Dark Sage

## Stuart France & Sue Vincent

.... something was spawned up on the moor... something black that flew on dark wings...It heeds not time or place...It seem to have developed a penchant for the travels of Don and Wen....

"Are those two still at it?"
"Apparently...."

The Dark Ages appear in the copybook pages of our historical records like an ink spot. An insidious black mark; a veritable blot on the landscape of time. There are some who claim they never actually existed and that the two hundred odd years represented by their darkness are a fabrication designed to fit the grandiose plotting of an ego-driven king. There are probably only two people mad enough to take such a notion seriously.

Across the Derbyshire landscape, scattered with sites of ancient sanctity and strange, otherworldly places, our two unlikely companions begin another chapter of their quest to understand the roots of human consciousness and the source of inner light that draws the eyes and heart towards to sun.

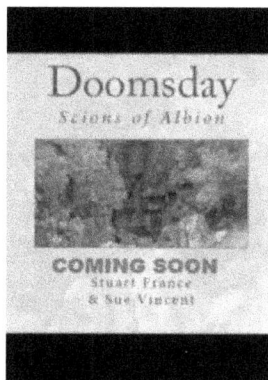

*The final book in the Doomsday Triad*

# Doomsday: Scions of Albion

## Stuart France and Sue Vincent

To be released in 2015

…"Just make sure there's enough room in the boot of the car," says Wen and throws me the keys to the Silver Bullet before disappearing back into the flat to retrieve something.

I peruse with some consternation those contents: a wheel-barrow, a spade, a crow bar and a length of rope and when I look up to remonstrate with Wen she appears to be clad head to foot in black, wearing a black balaclava on her head, and holding an air rifle.

"What the…"

"Just put that in the boot and get in the car," she says, handing me what can only be my own black balaclava and cladding.

"There had better be a damn good reason for all this," say I clambering into the front seat.

"Too right there should," intones Ben's familiar drawl as he emerges upright from his prostrate position along the back seat of the Silver Bullet.

Somewhat un-reassuringly he also appears to be wearing a black balaclava….

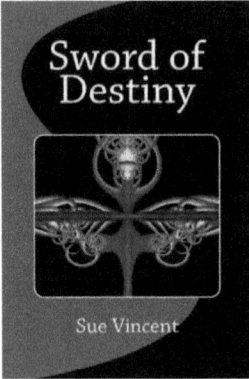

# SWORD OF DESTINY
## Sue Vincent

"...and the swords must be found and held by their bearers lest the darkness find a way into the heart of man. Ask the waters to grant guidance and tell the ancient Keeper of Light that it is time to join battle for the next age."

Rhea Marchant heads north to the wild and beautiful landscapes of the Yorkshire Dales where she is plunged into an adventure that will span the worlds. The earth beneath her feet reveals its hidden life as she and her companions are guided by the ancient Keeper of Light in search of artefacts of arcane power. With the aid of the Old Ones and the merry immortal Heilyn, the company seek the elemental weapons that will help restore hope to an unbalanced world at the dawn of a new era.

" Sue writes with a real grasp of the human side of people which is expressed in the personalities of her heroes and the recognizable characters that they interact with. The power and essence of her story is found in the admixture of her undoubted love of Yorkshire, her ability to see the warm and the good in all people, and her knowledge of the magical forces one can find at work in such places and between such folk. An inspired piece of writing that keeps your attention until the very last page."

*Dr G.M.Vasey, author of "The Last Observer" and "Inner Journeys: Explorations of the Soul ", co-author of "The Mystical Hexagram: The Seven Inner Stars of Power".*

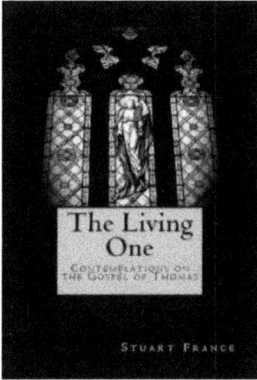

# THE LIVING ONE:

## Contemplations on the Gospel of Thomas

## Stuart France

**"...It is like the smallest of seeds and if it falls on prepared soil, it produces the largest of plants and shelters the birds of heaven..."**

Many scholars believe that the Gospel According to Thomas preserves a glimpse into the oral traditions of the Gospels. The book is a collection of sayings, parables and dialogues attributed to Jesus and forms part of the Nag Hammadi Library, a collection of ancient papyri found near the Dead Sea in 1945.

In this unique interpretation Stuart France brings the oral tradition to life, retelling the Gospel in his own words, in the way it may have been shared around the hearth fires of our forefathers. Deeply entwined with the story is the personal journey to understanding, following it down some rather unusual pathways. It begins with a road trip in an arid landscape far from home; a journey that led through a country that captured imagination and set it to music. It ends with an ancient story, told as you have never read it before.

**"Look, it's obvious, mozzies are God's Angels in disguise."**

Accompanied by a commentary which draws upon the esoteric traditions of the Mystery Schools, The Living One provides a new window on an age old story, being a transmutation of the spirit of the words, born of the personal realisations of a seeker after Truth.

> "Salome said to Joshua, "Who are you mister, you have eaten from my table and climbed on to my couch as if you are a stranger ?""

*Photography by Sue Vincent*

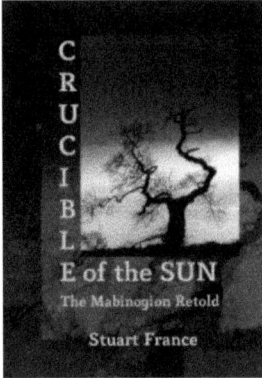

# CRUCIBLE OF THE SUN:

## The Mabinogion Retold

## By Stuart France

*"I will dazzle like fire, hard and high, will flame the breaths of my desire; chief revealer of that which is uttered and that which is asked, tonight I make naked the word."*

Once upon a time we gathered around the flames of the hearth and listened to tales of long ago and far away. The stories grew in the telling, weaving ancient lore whose origins lie somewhere in a misty past with tales of high adventure, battles, magic and love. In Crucible of the Sun this oral tradition is echoed in a unique and lyrical interpretation of tales from the Mabinogion, a collection of stories whose roots reach back into the depths of time, spanning the world and reflecting universal themes of myth and legend.

These tales capture a narrative deeply entwined through the history of the Celtic peoples of the British Isles, drawing on roots that are embedded in the heart of the land. In Crucible of the Sun the author retells these timeless stories in his own inimitable and eminently readable style. The author's deep exploration of the human condition and the transitions between the inner worlds illuminate this retelling, casting a unique light on the symbolism hidden beyond the words, unravelling the complex skein of imagery and weaving a rich tapestry of magic.

*Photography by Sue Vincent*

*'The author's creative and scholarly engagement with the material and enthusiasm for the original tales is evident throughout.' The Welsh Books Council*

*'I found it very inspiring!' Philip Carr-Gomm, Chosen Chief, Order of Bards, Ovates and Druids (O.B.O.D.)*

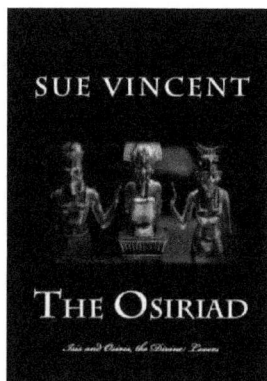

# THE OSIRIAD

## Isis & Osiris, the Divine Lovers

## Sue Vincent

**"There was a time we did not walk the earth. A time when our nascent essence flowed, undifferentiated, in the Source of Being."**

In forgotten ages, the stories tell, the gods lived and ruled amongst men. Many tales were told, across many times and cultures, following the themes common to all mankind. Stories were woven of love and loss, magic and mystery, life and death. One such story has survived from the most distant times. In the Two Lands of Ancient Egypt a mythical history has been preserved across millennia. It begins with the dawn of Creation itself and spans one of the greatest stories ever to capture the heart and imagination. Myths are, by their very nature, organic. They grow from a seed sown around a hearth fire, perhaps, and the stories travelled the ancient highways, embellished and adapted with each retelling. Who knows what the first story told?

In this retelling of the ancient story it is the Mistress of all Magic herself who tells the tale of the sacred family of Egypt.

"We have borne many names and many faces, my family and I. All races have called us after their own fashion and we live their stories for them, bringing to life the Universal Laws and Man's own innermost heart. We have laughed and loved, taught and suffered, sharing the emotions that give richness to life. But for now, I will share a chapter of my family's story. One that has survived intact through the millennia, known and remembered still, across your world. Carved in stone, written on papyrus, I will tell you of a time when my name was Isis."

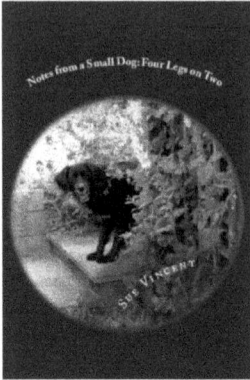

# NOTES FROM A SMALL DOG

## Four Legs on Two

### Sue Vincent

"He asked me what it is with balls…why I love them so much. I had a think about that. It is 'cause they fly. Like birds. I'm supposed to chase birds. I'm a bird-dog. 'Course, she won't really let me. It doesn't stop me barking at 'em and seeing 'em off from my garden. But it isn't the same. Somewhere, deep inside, I know what I am supposed to do, what I am supposed to be. But I can't be that for some reason… things aren't quite set up right for me to chase birds all day and bring them back to her. On the other hand, that's who I am…and you can't be anything else than that… so the balls let me be myself in a world where I can't catch birds all day.

She says that's not unusual… She seems to think that we all know who we really are, deep down, and that we spend all our time trying to find a way to be that in a world that doesn't quite seem to fit. We either find other stuff to express it…like balls…. Or we try and be what others think we should be… But you can't be a terrier if you are a retriever, can you? A bit like asking a fish to climb trees. It can be done, but it isn't easy!"

Ani, a very familiar spirit, was named for one of the ancient gods. It should, I suppose, have been no surprise when she took over the keyboard and began to write. A year later she had me collect her writings into a single volume at the insistence of her fans... who have been taken by her playful love of life and her odd wisdom...largely because she is saving for an automatic tennis ball launcher. The book is a collection of Ani's periodic posts. She even lets me write occasionally… By this time you may, of course, think I am barking mad myself… you may have a point… but I stand with Orhan Pamuk, "Dogs do speak, but only to those who know how to listen."

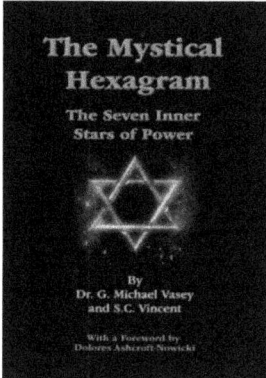

# THE MYSTICAL HEXAGRAM:

## The Seven Inner Stars of Power

## Dr G. Michael Vasey & S.C.Vincent

### Foreword by Dolores Ashcroft-Nowicki

The Mystical Hexagram is a new book by Dr G. Michael Vasey and S.C.Vincent. The book explores a symbol. Not from some scholarly or deeply complex perspective, but seeing it as a representation relating to life and living. The forces and pressures that are associated with the hexagram are, after all the forces of life at both practical and Universal levels. By exploring and beginning to understand the symbol, we are able to learn and discover more about ourselves.

The meditations throughout the book take you on an inner journey of exploration, discovering the parallels between the self and the greater reality within which we live our lives. They illustrate the connection between the inner and outer world of the self and the cosmic forces of Creation. Having traced that connecting path, the meditations offer a practical way of applying that understanding.

In addition to the exercises the book includes two very special meditations, The Garden of Remembrance and the Circle of Healing. These two you will want to revisit many times, taking away from the experience a sense of peace and beauty.

The book is now available through Datura Press

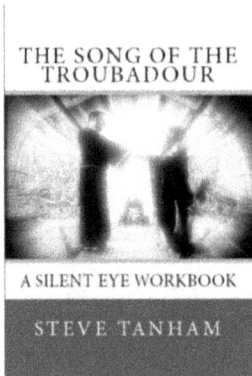

# THE SONG OF THE TROUBADOUR:

## A Silent Eye Workbook

## by Steve Tanham

*Foreword by Sue Vincent*

*With contributions from Stuart France and those who were there to share this very special journey.*

"Being is without beginning and end. This flowing, loving, intelligence is the basis of everything we know. Whatever level of consciousness we attain, it will only reveal the greater and greater depth of Being that has always been there within us and before us.

Being also forms the objects that we believe are separated from us. But the Reality and the Truth are that we live and have our own being in a sea of endless loving energy that is our true home. There is no separation, there is in the end, no journey; there is only realisation, and seeing. What unveils itself before us was always there."

A group of pilgrims have been brought together in the ancient monastery of the Keepers of the First Flame. Unexpectedly, the door opens and into their midst stride the Troubadours, holding a Child by the hand…. a very special Child in whom the Light of Being shines clear… and who can see the world as it really is…

Thus began the inaugural weekend that saw the Birthing of the Silent Eye, a modern Mystery School. This workbook is both a practical transcript of the dramatic rituals of that weekend and the story of that Birth. The book opens a window onto the workings of a modern Mystery school, sharing the accounts of some of those who attended the weekend as well as the detailed script of the powerful ritual drama. If you have ever wondered what really goes on… this book is for you.

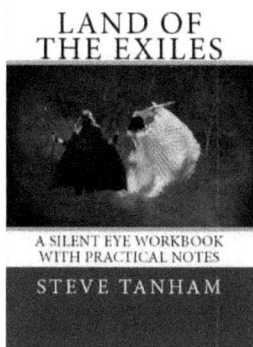

# Land of the Exiles

## A Silent Eye Workbook

## With Practical Notes

## By Steve Tanham

*With Contributions from Sue Vincent and Stuart France*

*and the Companions of the Hawk.*

In April 2014 the Silent Eye, a modern Mystery School, hosted the Land of the Exiles as a weekend workshop. These annual gatherings attract people from across the world to share a unique approach to the spiritual journey that is taken by all. Over the course of the workshop a story unfolds, dramatic and emotive, engaging the hearts and minds of the participants, shadowing forth the challenges of the inner journey to awakening. This workbook includes the script from that journey, along with practical and explanatory notes, as well as the personal accounts of some of the Companions who shared an epic journey of the imagination as a spaceship crash-lands on a far-flung planet, and a cyborg forces them to play out the story of the ancient gods of Egypt, intent of calculating just what it means to be human…

The Hawk has crash-landed on the planet Idos, the crew awake from cryogenic sleep to find that their captain is missing and the ship has been taken over by a cyborg who bends them to his will, making them play out the stories of the ancient gods of Egypt as it seeks to understand what it is to be human. Their only hope of survival lies in the strange touch of the Midstream, and their own inner hearts.

A practical guide to a fully scripted ritual workshop from the Silent Eye, a modern Mystery School.

www.ingramcontent.com/pod-product-compliance
Lightning Source LLC
Chambersburg PA
CBHW071847020426
42331CB00007B/1893